Winter 1998 Edition

COLLECTOR'S
VALUE GUIDE™

Collector Handbook and Price Guide

Ty®'s Beanie Babies™

Doodle   *Strut*

Collector's Name

Contents

Special thanks to Bears By The Sea, Pismo Beach, CA.

COLLECTOR'S VALUE GUIDE™ and THE COLLECTOR'S POCKET PLANNER™ are trademarks of Collectors' Publishing Co., Inc. The Collector's Value Guide™ is not affiliated with Ty Inc. or any of its affiliates, subsidiaries, distributors or representatives. Any opinions expressed are solely those of the authors, and do not necessarily reflect those of Ty Inc. Ty® is a registered trademark of Ty Inc. Beanie Babies™ and Pillow Pals™ are trademarks of Ty Inc. Product names and product designs are the property of Ty Inc., Oakbrook, IL. Illustrations are the original creations and property of Collectors' Publishing Co., Inc.

Front cover (background to foreground): "Gobbles™," "1997 Teddy™," "Snowball™," "Peace™," "Waddle™," "Seamore™."
Back cover (left to right): "Steg™," "Legs™," "Goldie™."

Managing Editor:	Jeff Mahony	Art Director:	Joe T. Nguyen
	jeff@collectorspub.com		*joe@collectorspub.com*
Associate Editor:	Jan Cronan	Staff Artists:	Scott Sierakowski
Editorial Assistants:	Gia C. Manalio		David Ten Eyck
	Melissa Bennett		Lance Doyle
Contributing Editor:	Mike Micciulla		

Illustrations by Joe T. Nguyen, David Ten Eyck and Sal LoNero.

ISBN 1-888914-14-9

Collectors' Publishing Co., Inc.
598 Pomeroy Avenue
Meriden, CT 06450
http://www.collectorspub.com

Introducing The Beanie Babies™ Value Guide

Welcome to the Winter 1998 Edition of the Beanie Babies™ Value Guide! Everyone is talking about Ty's Beanie Babies! They're irresistibly cute. They're next to impossible to find in stores. They're turning adults into Beanie bounty hunters. They're turning kids into Wall Street wheelers and dealers. They're all over the newspapers, the Internet and television newscasts. Who would have guessed that these tiny children's toys would become the hottest collectible to hit the country in years?

You may not know why you love Beanie Babies so much, but you *do* know that you want them all! And if you're hungry for Beanie Babies information, the Collector's Value Guide has it all!

★ *Full Color Pictures of all Beanies & Teenie Beanies!*

★ *October New Releases and Retirements!*

★ *Up-to-date Secondary Market Values!*

★ *The Latest News on Variations, Name Changes & More!*

★ *Feature Section on the Top Ten Most Valuable Beanies!*

★ *Room to Keep Track of your own Beanie Collection!*

★ *Complete Listing of Beanie Babies Poems!*

★ *Quizzes! Word Searches! Word Scrambles!*

★ *Also includes Ty's Pillow Pals!*

The easy-to-use Collector's Value Guide will make collecting Beanie Babies more fun than ever!

COLLECTOR'S
VALUE GUIDE™

Beanie Babies™ Overview

Early in 1994 – under the cover of darkness – a band of nine little beanbag animals crept into retail stores in the Midwest. Once inside, they arranged themselves on the shelves and waited to be discovered . . . and waited . . . and waited some more. Finally, people began to take notice of the adorable animals. Kids and adults alike couldn't resist those cute, floppy critters and pretty soon, the original nine were joined by even more of their friends. Word began to spread to other parts of the country and suddenly, by 1996, a low rumble heard all across the land turned into . . .

A Beanie Babies Explosion!

You can call Ty Inc.'s Beanie Babies the hottest collectible in the country or the wildest craze ever – you're right either way! From New York to Texas to Alaska, it seems as though *everyone* is talking about those delightful beanbag animals. The Internet crackles with Beanie electricity as collectors share their love for the plush critters; and Beanie Babies are not shy in the spotlight as they have also been the subject of articles in major newspapers all over the country and have appeared on national TV programs such as the "Today Show." But what's the whole Beanie Babies story? What's this craze all about? And where is it all going?

COLLECTOR'S
VALUE GUIDE™

Birth Of The Beanies

Beanie Babies are made by Ty Inc., which has been producing plush animals since 1985 (collectors may recall seeing the now-famous Ty logo on many different stuffed animals over the years). When Ty Warner, founder of the company, released the first Beanie Babies in early 1994, he knew he was offering a line of adorable beanbag animals that kids could afford – but he had no idea he was about to turn the entire country upside-down!

Generally, Ty introduces new Beanie Babies designs twice a year (in January and June), although in 1997 there were three releases in January, May and October. Retirement announcements are usually made at the same time as the new releases. Including the 34 new designs for 1997, a total of 126 Beanie Babies have been issued, with 77 of them currently available. In the collection, collectors will find all sorts of animals, from dogs, cats, bears and bunnies to more unusual animals such as "Batty" the bat, "Sting" the manta ray and "Kiwi" the toucan. There also are "fantasy" animals like "Mystic" the unicorn and "Magic" the dragon, not to mention three dinosaurs, a ghost and even a new snowman! There were also ten Teenie Beanie Babies produced for a special McDonald's promotion in April 1997 (see page 9).

Beanie Babies are produced in China and Korea. Every Beanie Babies animal begins as a plush pattern that is filled with small, round PVC pellets. The animals aren't filled completely, however – that's how they get their playful "floppiness." Also, because the Beanie Babies are individually sewn, rarely do any two of the same Beanie look exactly alike. There will always be minor tweaks in appearance, giving each Beanie its own unique personality. There also have been color and design variations on some Beanie Babies. For example, "Peanut" the elephant was changed from a dark blue to a light blue and "Quackers" the duck grew wings after being originally produced with no wings. For a complete survey of Beanie Babies variations, see *Variations* section starting on page 55.

Beanie Babies™ Overview

The Beanie Babies Phenomenon

It's been a long time since Americans have seen a craze as big as Ty's Beanie Babies, if ever. But what is it about them that have made them the hottest collectible in the country?

Beanie Babies Are FUN

Not only are Beanie Babies absolutely adorable, but they just HAVE to be played with! Kids all over the country are bringing "Waddle" the penguin, "Bessie" the cow or "Magic" the dragon to school; or they make playsets for their Beanie Babies in their bedrooms; or they create stories with their Beanies as the main characters. Even adults can't resist Beanie Babies: There are probably a lot of adults reading this sentence who have one, two or a whole pack of Beanies at their desks at work (and check the drawers of those who scoff at this)! For most Beanie Babies collectors, the name of the game has always been "fun!"

Beanie Babies Are AFFORDABLE

Beanie Babies generally cost between $5 to $8 at retail stores, which means Beanies are a whole lot of fun for only a little bit of money. This is especially appealing for kids with a weekly allowance (and also for those parents who are rediscovering the benefits of the weekly allowance such as beds being made and dishes being done). After all, in today's world with the disappearance of the five and dime, what can a youngster buy for under $10 that's as much fun as Beanie Babies? Meanwhile, collectors can add several pieces to their Beanie Babies collections in one trip to the store and *still* spend less than $25.

Beanie Babies Are HARD TO FIND

It might seem strange, but the fact that the Beanie Babies can be hard to find in stores actually helps increase the popularity – and the value – of Beanie Babies. Even these cuddly critters aren't exempt from the laws of supply and demand. Before the collection took off in popularity, most

COLLECTOR'S
VALUE GUIDE™

Beanies were readily available in retail stores. But that all changed around the fall of 1996, when demand suddenly outgrew the supply. The result? Retailers can't get enough Beanies for their shelves and many collectors end up buying whichever Beanies they see in the store. It might not be the exact one they were looking for, but the old saying "beggars can't be choosers" is something Beanie collectors can relate to! This incredible demand translates into Beanie Babies fever and great anticipation for future releases.

Tagging Along

A big part of the Beanie Babies' appeal can be found in the heart-shaped hang tags (also referred to as "heart tags" or "swing tags") attached to the animals. These tags have been with the Beanies since the beginning, although they have changed slightly over the years (see *Ty Tags* section on page 61 for an in-depth look at hang tag variations).

On the tags you will learn everything there is to know about that Beanie. Each tag lists the animal's name and style number. And in 1996, the tags began to list the animals' birthdates. Not only did this give the collector a reason to celebrate but it also presented the challenge of finding those Beanies who share the birthdays of family members and friends. And adding to the fun in 1996 was the introduction of poems on the tags. These fun verses give life to the Beanie Babies with lines such as "Daisy drinks milk each night/So her coat is shiny and bright" and "Inky's head is big and round/As he swims he makes no sound."

The hang tags are the best way to determine an authentic Ty Beanie Babies animal from one of the several varieties of "imitation" Beanies that have popped up over the last year or so. These Beanie look-alikes are produced by other companies and shouldn't be confused with true Beanie Babies bearing the Ty hang tag.

Beanie Babies™ Overview

In addition to the hang tags, Beanie Babies also have tush tags, which are fabric tags sewn into the back ends of the characters. These tags have also changed over the years.

The Internet Connection

Collectors all over the country have turned the Internet into their personal Beanie Babies playground! Since Ty Inc. keeps a low profile in regards to advertising, word of mouth via the Internet has been the biggest source of Beanie news.

Ty Inc. has its own website (*www.ty.com*) where collectors can keep up with new releases and retirements, play games, get e-mail addresses of other Beanie collectors and much more. Stop in daily at the site to read the Beanie Babies "Quote of the Day" and share the secrets of the featured Beanies' internet diary. And don't forget to check out the "Beanie Of The Month" – this critter could be a member of your very own collection! But if you do a little looking, you'll find an entirely different world of Beanie information waiting for you! There are literally thousands of websites maintained by retailers and collectors where adults and kids hungry for Beanie information share what they know about color variations, differences in hang tags, etc. Collectors can buy, sell or trade their Beanies, participate in on-line auctions, join clubs or just "talk Beanies" in chat rooms or on bulletin boards visited by thousands of Beanie collectors each day. You never know exactly what you'll find on the Internet! And as always, a word of caution: while the Internet is a great source of Beanie information, you can't always believe what you read and collectors should be careful about the information they receive on-line, especially when buying and selling Beanie Babies on the secondary market.

COLLECTOR'S
VALUE GUIDE™

8

Teenie Beanie Invasion

What started as an innocent, fun promotion in April 1997 quickly turned into a collector feeding frenzy when McDonald's offered a series of "Teenie Beanie Babies™" as toys in their Happy Meals. These ten pieces were smaller versions of existing Beanies and were available only from the Happy Meal promotion. Once collectors got wind of it, they descended on McDonald's all over the country, sometimes buying dozens of meals at a time in order to get the complete set. The promotion was scheduled to run from April 11 through May 15, but supplies were wiped out so quickly that it was cut short after only two weeks! Ty hasn't announced whether there will be another McDonald's promotion, but rumors have circulated that there may be one in the works. So given the incredible popularity of the Teenie Beanies, it would be a good idea for collectors to keep their eyes, ears and appetites open!

How Long Will It Last?

Coping with the Beanie craze has been at times frustrating for both collectors and retailers. Because the demand for Beanies has been so overwhelming, Ty Inc. limits the number of Beanies each store can order. Some stores are still waiting for Beanies they ordered six months ago – which means collectors have to wait as well. Many store owners field dozens of calls every day from collectors asking if the Beanie Babies are in stock, and if so, which ones? Some stores suffering from "Beanie burnout" actually have answering machines featuring messages saying, "If you are calling for any reason OTHER than Beanie Babies . . ."

So, what's next on the Ty frontier? Some retailers are reporting brisk sales for Ty's Pillow Pals line of larger, washable plush companions (see section on pages 76-77). Some of these critters even resemble their smaller Beanie Babies buddies!

Many people wonder how long this Beanie Babies craze will last. No one knows for certain, but it's safe to say that a Beanie Babies animal that is cute and fun today will still be cute and fun five years from now!

COLLECTOR'S
VALUE GUIDE™

What's New

Introducing The October 1, 1997 Releases!

The Beanie Babies collection keeps on growing with 5 new releases in October of 1997, bringing the total number of releases to 126. Among these irresistible bean-filled pals, collectors will find a fine assortment of holiday-related Beanie treats!

1997 Teddy™ . . . As "Teddy," the last of the new-face color bears retires, the Beanies welcome the newest member of their teddy family, the "1997 Teddy" to their holiday celebration. With his Santa cap and red and green ribbons tied around his neck, this would-be St. Nick offers holiday cheer to all.

1997 Teddy

Batty™ . . . "Batty" flies into the Beanie collection just in time for Halloween to take over ruling the night skies from his retired pal and mentor, "Radar." But never fear as from the looks of this soft pink critter, the only things he likes to sink his fangs into are strawberry milkshakes.

Batty

Gobbles™ . . . Collectors will be giving thanks if they are lucky enough to get their hands on "Gobbles." As the first bird of its kind on the Beanie farm, this brown and red turkey is sure to be gobbled up quickly by Beanie enthusiasts.

Gobbles

Snowball™ . . . It's wintertime and what better way to usher in the new season than with the introduction of the first Beanie Babies snowman. "Snowball" makes a dapper debut in his bright red scarf and black top hat with matching red band.

Snowball

Spinner™ . . . Poor "Spinner"–he tries so hard to lurk in the darkness as he spins his web, but his orange stripes always give him away. He wonders if his retired friend "Web" ever had this problem.

Spinner

There have been 46 Beanie Babies designs officially retired by Ty. In 1997, Ty announced seven retirements on its website (www.ty.com) on January 1st, nine on May 11th and another 11 on October 1st. A great way to keep informed about potential retirements is by monitoring Ty's much-visited website. In addition to the retirements, there have been three pieces that have undergone name changes with the original versions no longer available. "Brownie" was discontinued, only to re-appear as "Cubbie," "Nana" became "Bongo" and "Doodle" became "Strut." The ten Teenie Beanie Babies designs that were available at McDonald's restaurants were sold out by April 25, 1997 (even earlier in some parts of the country).

Introducing The October 1, 1997 Retirements!

○ Ally, *alligator*   ● Bessie, *cow*   ● Flip, *cat*

○ Hoot, *owl*   ● Legs, *frog*   ● Seamore, *seal*

○ Speedy, *turtle*   ● Spot, *dog*   ○ Tank, *armadillo*

● Teddy, *brown bear*   ○ Velvet, *panther*   *How many do you have?*

Retirements

Retired in 1995 & 1996 . . .
- Bronty, *brontosaurus*
- Bumble, *bee*
- Caw, *crow*
- Chilly, *polar bear*
- Flutter, *butterfly*
- Humphrey, *camel*
- Peking, *panda*
- Rex, *tyrannosaurus*
- Slither, *snake*
- Steg, *stegosaurus*
- Teddy, *cranberry bear*
- Teddy, *jade bear*
- Teddy, *magenta bear*
- Teddy, *teal bear*
- Teddy, *violet bear*
- Trap, *mouse*
- Web, *spider*

Retired on January 1, 1997 . . .
- Chops, *lamb*
- Coral, *tropical fish*
- Kiwi, *toucan*
- Lefty, *donkey with flag*
- Libearty, *bear with flag*
- Righty, *elephant with flag*
- Sting, *manta ray*
- Tabasco, *bull*
- Tusk, *walrus*

Retired on May 11, 1997 . . .
- Bubbles, *tropical fish*
- Digger, *crab*
- Flash, *dolphin*
- Garcia, *bear*
- Grunt, *razorback*
- Manny, *manatee*
- Radar, *bat*
- Sparky, *dalmatian*
- Splash, *orca whale*

Retired on October 1, 1997 . . .
- Ally, *alligator*
- Bessie, *cow*
- Flip, *cat*
- Hoot, *owl*
- Legs, *frog*
- Seamore, *seal*
- Speedy, *turtle*
- Spot, *dog*
- Tank, *armadillo*
- Teddy, *brown bear*
- Velvet, *panther*

TEENIE BEANIE BABIES™ Retired in April 1997 . . .
- Chocolate, *moose*
- Chops, *lamb*
- Goldie, *goldfish*
- Lizz, *lizard*
- Patti, *platypus*
- Pinky, *flamingo*
- Quacks, *duck*
- Seamore, *seal*
- Snort, *bull*
- Speedy, *turtle*

This section spotlights the ten most valuable Beanie Babies based on their secondary market values. Because market prices can fluctuate, even over a short period of time, these rankings can change quickly! If you have *any* of them in your Beanie Babies collection, you're one lucky collector!

Some of these are color or design variations (see *Variations* section beginning on page 55), while others are simply older and harder to find. Either way, these are the ten crown jewels for Beanie Babies fanatics!

#1

PEANUT (dark blue) – $1700

This sought-after variation was shipped only in the month of July 1995 before changing to light blue, making it the rarest of all!

#2

QUACKERS (without wings) – $1500

Originally, "Quackers" was produced without wings. There may be less than 1,000 wingless "Quackers" in existence.

#3

SPOT (without spot) – $1300

Surprising but true, this very appropriately-named puppy was first produced without the now-familiar spot on his back.

#4

ZIP (all black) – $1250

An all-black version of "Zip" was produced in 1995 for a very short time. There are two other unique versions of this Beanie.

#5

HUMPHREY – $850

Although "Humphrey" was available for two years, he may have been too "unique" for collectors' tastes. That's changed now!

#6

CHILLY – $810

Only available for one year, "Chilly" is a difficult find, especially with his white fur in good condition.

#7

NANA – $800

"Bongo" was first produced in 1995 with the name "Nana" on the hang tag. "Nana" has a brown tail like early versions of "Bongo."

#8

BROWNIE – $790

The bear now known as "Cubbie" was originally produced with the name "Brownie" on the hang tag in 1994.

#9

PEKING – $685

Only available for one year, the exotic "Peking" was one of only four bears designed to lie on his stomach.

#10

TEDDY (teal, new face) – $670

This teal-colored version of "Teddy" features a rounded snout as opposed to its original more "pointed" appearance.

How To Use Your Value Guide

The Beanie Babies are pictured in this section in alphabetical order (Teenie Beanies are listed separately at the end of the section), so it will be very easy for you to find the Beanies in your collection. The October Beanie releases are listed on page 16. The information you will find on each Beanie includes the name, animal type, birthdate, issue year and whether the Beanie is current or retired. You can check off the *"Got it!"* circle for the ones you already have and fill in the price you paid.

If you're interested in the secondary market, it's easy to figure out the value of your own Beanie collection:

1. First, find the value of your Beanie on the "Market Value" line. For Beanies with variations, look carefully at the pictures to determine which version you own.

2. Then, write the total of the Beanies you have on each page in the "Value Totals" box. For current pieces, simply fill in the price you paid on the "Market Value" line.

3. Finally, go to page 52 and write in the totals from each page to get the grand total of the value of your Beanie Babies collection! Make sure you use a pencil because every time you buy a Beanie, you'll want to record its value and watch the grand total grow!

Keep in mind that because Beanie Babies are a relatively new "collectible," secondary market values may rise or fall rapidly. Note: The "Original 9" designs are marked by an asterisk (*); these Beanie Babies may have appeared in some stores in late 1993.

Bongo™
Monkey • Born: 8-17-95
Issued: 1995 • Current
○ *Got it!* • Paid: $____
Market Value:
a. *Tan tail* – $____
b. *Brown tail* – $80
c. *"Nana" variation* – $800

New   #4200

1997 Teddy™
Bear • Born: N/A
Issued: 1997 • Current
● *Got it!* • Paid: $____
Market Value: $____

New   #4035

Batty™
Bat • Born: N/A
Issued: 1997 • Current
○ *Got it!* • Paid: $____
Market Value: $____

New   #4034

Gobbles™
Turkey • Born: N/A
Issued: 1997 • Current
● *Got it!* • Paid: $____
Market Value: $____

New   #4201

Snowball™
Snowman • Born: N/A
Issued: 1997 • Current
○ *Got it!* • Paid: $____
Market Value: $____

New   #4036

Spinner™
Spider • Born: N/A
Issued: 1997 • Current
○ *Got it!* • Paid: $____
Market Value: $____

Value Totals _____

1   #4032

Retired October 1997

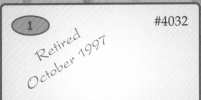

Ally™
Alligator • Born: 3-14-94
Issued: 1994 • ~~Current~~
○ *Got it!* • Paid: $____
Market Value: $ 40

2   #4074

Baldy™
Eagle • Born: 2-17-96
Issued: 1997 • Current
○ *Got it!* • Paid: $____
Market Value: $____

3   #4109

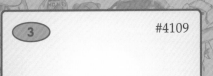

Bernie™
St. Bernard • Born: 10-3-96
Issued: 1997 • Current
○ *Got it!* • Paid: $____
Market Value: $____

4   #4009

Retired October 1997

Bessie™
Cow • Born: 6-27-95
Issued: 1995 • ~~Current~~
● *Got it!* • Paid: $____
Market Value: $ 50

COLLECTOR'S
VALUE GUIDE™

Value
Totals _____

5   #4011

Blackie™
Bear • Born 7-15-94
Issued: 1994 • Current
⬤ *Got it!* • Paid: $____
Market Value: $____

6   #4163

Blizzard™
Tiger • Born: 12-12-96
Issued: 1997 • Current
⬤ *Got it!* • Paid: $____
Market Value: $____

7   #4001

Bones™
Dog • Born: 1-18-94
Issued: 1994 • Current
○ *Got it!* • Paid: $____
Market Value: $____

8   #4067

a
b
c

Bongo™
Monkey • Born: 8-17-95
Issued: 1995 • Current
○ *Got it!* • Paid: $____
Market Value:
a. *Tan tail* – $____
b. *Brown tail* – $80
c. *"Nana" variation* – $800

**Value
Totals** _____

COLLECTOR'S
VALUE GUIDE™

9   #4085

Bronty™
Brontosaurus • Born: N/A
Issued: 1995 • Retired: 1996
○ *Got it!* • Paid: $_____
Market Value: **$425**

10   #4010

Brownie™
(name changed to "Cubbie" in 1994)
Bear • Born: N/A
Issued: 1994*
Out of Production 1994
○ *Got it!* • Paid: $_____
Market Value: **$790**
* one of the "Original 9"

11   #4078

Bubbles™
Fish • Born 7-2-95
Issued: 1995 • Retired: 1997
○ *Got it!* • Paid: $_____
Market Value: **$50**

12   #4016

Bucky™
Beaver • Born: 6-8-95
Issued: 1996 • Current
● *Got it!* • Paid: $_____
Market Value: $_____

Value
Totals _____

13   #4045

Bumble™
Bee • Born: 10-16-95
Issued: 1995 • Retired 1996
○ *Got it!* • Paid: $____
Market Value: **$190**

14   #4071

Caw™
Crow • Born: N/A
Issued: 1995 • Retired: 1996
○ *Got it!* • Paid: $____
Market Value: **$200**

15   #4012

Chilly™
Polar Bear • Born: N/A
Issued: 1995 • Retired: 1996
○ *Got it!* • Paid: $____
Market Value: **$810**

16   #4121

Chip™
Cat • Born 1-26-96
Issued: 1997 • Current
○ *Got it!* • Paid: $____
Market Value: $____

Value Totals _____

COLLECTOR'S
VALUE GUIDE™

17 #4015

Chocolate™
Moose • Born: 4-27-93
Issued: 1994* • Current
◉ *Got it!* • Paid: $____
Market Value: $____
* one of the "Original 9"

18 #4019

Chops™
Lamb • Born: 5-3-96
Issued: 1996 • Retired: 1997
○ *Got it!* • Paid: $____
Market Value: **$75**

19 #4083

Claude™
Crab • Born: 9-3-96
Issued: 1997 • Current
○ *Got it!* • Paid: $____
Market Value: $____

20 #4160

Congo™
Gorilla • Born: 11-9-96
Issued: 1996 • Current
◉ *Got it!* • Paid: $____
Market Value: $____

COLLECTOR'S
VALUE GUIDE™

Value
Totals _____

21 #4079

Coral™
Fish • Born 3-2-95
Issued: 1995 • Retired: 1997
○ *Got it!* • Paid: $____
Market Value: **$75**

22 #4130

Crunch™
Shark • Born: 1-13-96
Issued: 1997 • Current
○ *Got it!* • Paid: $____
Market Value: $____

23 #4010

b

a

Cubbie™
Bear • Born: 11-14-93
Issued: 1994* • Current
○ *Got it!* • Paid: $____
Market Value:
a. *"Cubbie"* – $____
b. *"Brownie" variation* – **$725**
* one of the "Original 9"

24 #4052

Curly™
Bear • Born: 4-12-96
Issued: 1996 • Current
◉ *Got it!* • Paid: $____
Market Value: $____

Value
Totals _____

25 #4006

Daisy™
Cow • Born: 5-10-94
Issued: 1994 • Current
● *Got it!* • Paid: $____
Market Value: $____

26 #4008

a

b

Derby™
Horse • Born: 9-16-95
Issued: 1995 • Current
● *Got it!* • Paid: $____
Market Value:
a. *Coarse mane & tail* – $____
b. *Fine mane & tail* – **$400**

27 #4027

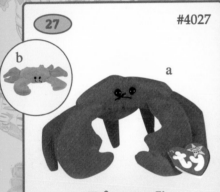

b

a

Digger™
Crab • Born: 8-23-95
Issued: 1995 • Retired: 1997
○ *Got it!* • Paid: $____
Market Value:
a. *Red* – **$50**
b. *Orange* – **$340**

28 #4110

Doby™
Doberman • Born: 10-9-96
Issued: 1997 • Current
● *Got it!* • Paid: $____
Market Value: $____

COLLECTOR'S
VALUE GUIDE™

Value	
Totals	_____

29 #4171

Doodle™
(name changed to "Strut" in 1997)
Rooster • Born: 3-8-96
Issued: 1997
Out of Production 1997
○ *Got it!* • Paid: $____
Market Value: **$55**

30 #4100

Dotty™
Dalmatian • Born: 10-17-96
Issued: 1997 • Current
● *Got it!* • Paid: $____
Market Value: $____

31 #4018

Ears™
Bunny • Born: 4-18-95
Issued: 1996 • Current
● *Got it!* • Paid: $____
Market Value: $____

32 #4180

Echo™
Dolphin • Born: 12-21-96
Issued: 1997 • Current
○ *Got it!* • Paid: $____
Market Value: $____

Value Totals _____

COLLECTOR'S
VALUE GUIDE™

33   #4021

Flash™
Dolphin • Born: 5-13-93
Issued: 1994* • Retired: 1997
○ *Got it!* • Paid: $____
Market Value: **$50**
* one of the "Original 9"

34   #4125

Fleece™
Lamb • Born: 3-21-96
Issued: 1997 • Current
● *Got it!* • Paid: $____
Market Value: $____

35   #4012

Retired October 1997

Flip™
Cat • Born: 2-28-95
Issued: 1996 • ~~Current~~
● *Got it!* • Paid: $____
Market Value: $_40_

36   #4118

Floppity™
Bunny • Born: 5-28-96
Issued: 1997 • Current
● *Got it!* • Paid: $____
Market Value: $____

COLLECTOR'S
VALUE GUIDE™

Value Totals	_____

37 — #4043

Flutter™
Butterfly • Born: N/A
Issued: 1995 • Retired: 1996
○ *Got it!* • Paid: $____
Market Value: **$425**

38 — #4066

Freckles™
Leopard • Born: 6-3-96
Issued: 1996 • Current
◉ *Got it!* • Paid: $____
Market Value: $____

39 — #4051

Garcia™
Bear • Born: 8-1-95
Issued: 1996 • Retired: 1997
○ *Got it!* • Paid: $____
Market Value: **$80**

40 — #4023

Goldie™
Goldfish • Born: 11-14-94
Issued: 1994 • Current
○ *Got it!* • Paid: $____
Market Value: $____

Value
Totals _____

COLLECTOR'S
VALUE GUIDE™

41   #4126

Gracie™
Swan • Born: 6-17-96
Issued: 1997 • Current
◐ *Got it!* • Paid: $____
Market Value: $____

42   #4092

Grunt™
Razorback • Born: 7-19-95
Issued: 1996 • Retired: 1997
○ *Got it!* • Paid: $____
Market Value: **$65**

43   #4061

b

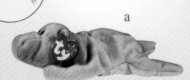

a

Happy™
Hippo • Born: 2-25-94
Issued: 1994 • Current
◐ *Got it!* • Paid: $____
Market Value:
  a. *Lavender* – $____
  b. *Gray* – **$330**

44   #4119

Hippity™
Bunny • Born: 6-1-96
Issued: 1997 • Current
◐ *Got it!* • Paid: $____
Market Value: $____

Value
Totals _____

45   #4073

Retired October 1997

Hoot™
Owl • Born: 8-9-95
Issued: 1996 • ~~Current~~
○ *Got it!* • Paid: $____
Market Value: $_40_

46   #4117

Hoppity™
Bunny • Born: 4-3-96
Issued: 1997 • Current
● *Got it!* • Paid: $____
Market Value: $____

47   #4060

Humphrey™
Camel • Born: N/A
Issued: 1994 • Retired: 1996
○ *Got it!* • Paid: $____
Market Value: $850

48   #4044

b

a

Inch™
Worm • Born: 9-3-95
Issued: 1995 • Current
○ *Got it!* • Paid: $____
Market Value:
a. *Yarn antennae* – $____
b. *Felt antennae* – $120

**Value
Totals** _____

COLLECTOR'S
VALUE GUIDE™

49   #4028

Inky™
Octopus • Born: 11-29-94
Issued: 1994 • Current
Got it! • Paid: $_____
Market Value:
  a. *Pink* – $_____
  b. *Tan* – **$295**

50   #4082

Jolly™
Walrus • Born: 12-2-96
Issued: 1997 • Current
○ Got it! • Paid: $_____
Market Value: $_____

51   #4070

Kiwi™
Toucan • Born: 9-16-95
Issued: 1995 • Retired: 1997
○ Got it! • Paid: $_____
Market Value: **$70**

52   #4085

Lefty™
Donkey • Born: 7-4-96
Issued: 1996 • Retired: 1997
○ Got it! • Paid: $_____
Market Value: **$80**

COLLECTOR'S
VALUE GUIDE™

Value Totals	_____

53 #4020

Retired October 1997

Legs™
Frog • Born: 4-25-93
Issued: 1994* • ~~Current~~
● *Got it!* • Paid: $____
Market Value: $ 40
* one of the "Original 9"

54 #4057

Libearty™
Bear • Born: Summer 1996
Issued: 1996 • Retired: 1997
○ *Got it!* • Paid: $____
Market Value: **$85**

55 #4033

b

a

Lizzy™
Lizard • Born: 5-11-95
Issued: 1995 • Current
● *Got it!* • Paid: $____
Market Value:
a. *Blue/yellow* – $____
b. *Tie-dye* – $385

56 #4040

a

b

c

Lucky™
Ladybug • Born: 5-1-95
Issued: 1994 • Current
○ *Got it!* • Paid: $____
Market Value:
a. *11 sewn-on spots* – $____
b. *21 sewn-on spots* – $15
c. *7 glued-on spots* – $105

Value Totals _____

57 #4088

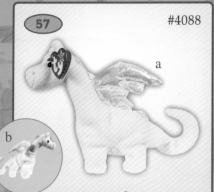

Magic™
Dragon • Born: 9-5-95
Issued: 1995 • Current
👁 *Got it!* • Paid: $____
Market Value:
a. *Pale pink thread* – $____
b. *Hot pink thread* – **$50**

58 #4081

Manny™
Manatee • Born: 6-8-95
Issued: 1996 • Retired: 1997
○ *Got it!* • Paid: $____
Market Value: **$65**

59 #4600

Maple™
Canadian Bear • Born: 7-1-96
Issued: 1997 • Current
○ *Got it!* • Paid: $____
Market Value:
a. *"Maple" tush tag* – $____
b. *"Pride" tush tag* – **$180**

60 #4162

Mel™
Koala • Born: 1-15-96
Issued: 1997 • Current
👁 *Got it!* • Paid: $____
Market Value: $____

Value
Totals _____

61   #4007

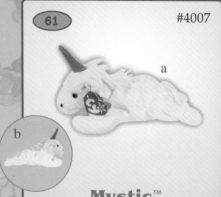

a

b

Mystic™
Unicorn • Born: 5-21-94
Issued: 1994 • Current
⊛ *Got it!* • Paid: $_____
Market Value:
a. *Coarse mane & tail – $_____*
b. *Fine mane & tail – $150*

---

62   #4067

Nana™
(name changed to "Bongo" in 1995)
Monkey • Born: N/A
Issued: 1995
Out of Production 1995
○ *Got it!* • Paid: $_____
Market Value: **$800**

---

63   #4104

Nanook™
Husky • Born: 11-21-96
Issued: 1997 • Current
⊛ *Got it!* • Paid: $_____
Market Value: $_____

---

64   #4003

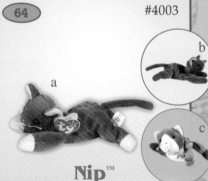

a

b

c

Nip™
Cat • Born: 3-6-94
Issued: 1994 • Current
⊛ *Got it!* • Paid: $_____
Market Value:
a. *Gold body/white paws – $_____*
b. *All gold – $635*
c. *White belly & face – $225*

Value Totals _____

65 #4114

Nuts™

Squirrel • Born: 1-21-96
Issued: 1997 • Current
◉ *Got it!* • Paid: $____
Market Value: $____

66 #4025

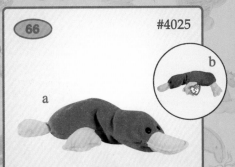

a

Patti™

Platypus • Born: 1-6-93
Issued: 1994* • Current
○ *Got it!* • Paid: $____
Market Value:
a. *Purple* – $____
b. *Magenta* – **$600**
* one of the "Original 9"

67 #4053

Peace™

Bear • Born: 2-1-96
Issued: 1997 • Current
○ *Got it!* • Paid: $____
Market Value: $____

68 #4062

a

b

Peanut™

Elephant • Born: 1-25-95
Issued: 1995 • Current
◉ *Got it!* • Paid: $____
Market Value:
~a. *Light blue* – $____
b. *Dark blue* – **$1700**

COLLECTOR'S VALUE GUIDE™

Value Totals _____

69 — #4013

Peking™
Panda • Born: N/A
Issued: 1994 • Retired: 1996
○ *Got it!* • Paid: $_____
Market Value: **$685**

70 — #4026

Pinchers™
Lobster • Born: 6-19-93
Issued: 1994* • Current
○ *Got it!* • Paid: $_____
Market Value: $_____
* one of the "Original 9"

71 — #4072

Pinky™
Flamingo • Born: 2-13-95
Issued: 1995 • Current
◉ *Got it!* • Paid: $_____
Market Value: $_____

72 — #4161

Pouch™
Kangaroo • Born: 11-6-96
Issued: 1997 • Current
◉ *Got it!* • Paid: $_____
Market Value: $_____

Value Totals _____

COLLECTOR'S
VALUE GUIDE™

73   #4106

Pugsly™
Pug • Born: 5-2-96
Issued: 1997 • Current
● *Got it!* • Paid: $____
Market Value: $____

74   #4024

a

b

Quackers™
Duck • Born: 4-19-94
Issued: 1994 • Current
○ *Got it!* • Paid: $____
Market Value:
a. *With wings* – $____
b. *Without wings* – **$1500**

75   #4091

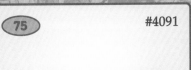

Radar™
Bat • Born: 10-30-95
Issued: 1995 • Retired: 1997
○ *Got it!* • Paid: $____
Market Value: **$75**

76   #4086

Rex™
Tyrannosaurus • Born: N/A
Issued: 1995 • Retired: 1996
○ *Got it!* • Paid: $____
Market Value: **$290**

COLLECTOR'S
VALUE GUIDE™

Value
Totals _____

77   #4086

Righty™
Elephant • Born: 7-4-96
Issued: 1996 • Retired: 1997
○ *Got it!* • Paid: $_____
Market Value: **$80**

78   #4014

Ringo™
Raccoon • Born: 7-14-95
Issued: 1996 • Current
○ *Got it!* • Paid: $_____
Market Value: $_____

79   #4069

Roary™
Lion • Born: 2-20-96
Issued: 1997 • Current
● *Got it!* • Paid: $_____
Market Value: $_____

80   #4101

Rover™
Dog • Born: 5-30-96
Issued: 1996 • Current
○ *Got it!* • Paid: $_____
Market Value: $_____

Value Totals _____

COLLECTOR'S
VALUE GUIDE™

81 #4107

Scoop™
Pelican • Born: 7-1-96
Issued: 1996 • Current
○ *Got it!* • Paid: $____
Market Value: $____

82 #4102

Scottie™
Scottish Terrier • Born: 6-15-96
Issued: 1996 • Current
◉ *Got it!* • Paid: $____
Market Value: $____

83 #4029

Retired
October 1997

Seamore™
Seal • Born: 12-14-96
Issued: 1994 • ~~Current~~
◉ *Got it!* • Paid: $____
Market Value: $_40_

84 #4080

Seaweed™
Otter • Born: 3-19-96
Issued: 1996 • Current
○ *Got it!* • Paid: $____
Market Value: $____

COLLECTOR'S
VALUE GUIDE™

Value
Totals _____

85 #4031

Slither™
Snake • Born: N/A
Issued: 1994 • Retired: 1996
○ *Got it!* • Paid: $____
Market Value: **$600**

86 #4115

a
b

Sly™
Fox • Born: 9-12-96
Issued: 1996 • Current
○ *Got it!* • Paid: $____
Market Value:
a. *White belly* – $____
b. *Brown belly* – **$100**

87 #4120

Snip™
Siamese Cat • Born: 10-22-96
Issued: 1997 • Current
○ *Got it!* • Paid: $____
Market Value: $____

88 #4002

Snort™
Bull • Born: 5-15-95
Issued: 1997 • Current
○ *Got it!* • Paid: $____
Market Value: $____

Value Totals _____

COLLECTOR'S
VALUE GUIDE™

89   #4100

Sparky™
Dalmatian • Born: 2-27-96
Issued: 1996 • Retired: 1997
○ *Got it!* • Paid: $_____
Market Value: **$50**

90   #4030

Retired October 1997

Speedy™
Turtle • Born: 8-14-94
Issued: 1994 • ~~Current~~
○ *Got it!* • Paid: $_____
Market Value: $ _40_

91   #4060

Spike™
Rhinoceros • Born: 8-13-96
Issued: 1996 • Current
○ *Got it!* • Paid: $_____
Market Value: $_____

92   #4022

Splash™
Whale • Born: 7-8-93
Issued: 1994* • Retired: 1997
○ *Got it!* • Paid: $_____
Market Value: **$50**
* one of the "Original 9"

Value
Totals _____

93   #4090

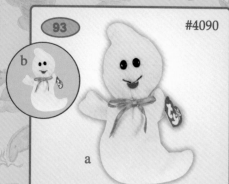

Spooky™
Ghost • Born: 10-31-95
Issued: 1995 • Current
○ *Got it!* • Paid: $____
Market Value:
a. *"Spooky" tag* – $____
b. *"Spook" tag* – **$150**

94   #4000

Retired October 1997

a

Spot™
Dog • Born: 1-3-93
Issued: 1994* • ~~Current~~
◉ *Got it!* • Paid: $____
Market Value:
a. *With spot on back* – $ 45
b. *Without spot* – **$1300**
* one of the "Original 9"

95   #4005

Squealer™
Pig • Born: 4-23-93
Issued: 1994* • Current
◉ *Got it!* • Paid: $____
Market Value: $____
* one of the "Original 9"

96   #4087

Steg™
Stegosaurus • Born: N/A
Issued: 1995 • Retired: 1996
○ *Got it!* • Paid: $____
Market Value: **$310**

Value Totals _____

97   #4077

Sting™
Manta Ray • Born: 8-27-95
Issued: 1995 • Retired: 1997
○ *Got it!* • Paid: $____
Market Value: **$75**

98   #4017

Stinky™
Skunk • Born: 2-13-95
Issued: 1995 • Current
○ *Got it!* • Paid: $____
Market Value: $____

99   #4065

Stripes™
Tiger • Born: 6-11-95
Issued: 1995 • Current
◉ *Got it!* • Paid: $____
Market Value:
  a. *Light orange* – $____
  b. *Dark orange* – **$180**
c. *Dark orange/fuzzy belly* – **$110**

100   #4171

Strut™
Rooster • Born: 3-8-96
Issued: 1997 • Current
○ *Got it!* • Paid: $____
Market Value:
  a. *"Strut"* – $____
b. *"Doodle" variation* – **$55**

COLLECTOR'S
VALUE GUIDE™

Value
Totals _____

101   #4002

Tabasco™
Bull • Born: 5-15-95
Issued: 1995 • Retired: 1997
○ *Got it!* • Paid: $_____
Market Value: **$200**

102   #4031

Retired October 1997

a   b   c

Tank™
Armadillo • Born: 2-22-95
Issued: 1996 • ~~Current~~
○ *Got it!* • Paid: $_____
Market Value:
a. *9 plates, with shell* – $_55_
b. *9 plates, no shell* – **$115**
c. *7 plates, no shell* – **$95**

103   #4050

a   b

Retired October 1997

Teddy™
Brown Bear • Born: 11-28-95
Issued: 1994 • ~~Current~~
● *Got it!* • Paid: $_____
Market Value:
a. *New face* – $_60_
b. *Old face* – **$575**

104   #4052

a   b

Teddy™
Cranberry Bear • Born: N/A
Issued: 1994 • Retired: 1995
○ *Got it!* • Paid: $_____
Market Value:
a. *New face* – **$450**
b. *Old face* – **$500**

Value Totals _____

COLLECTOR'S
VALUE GUIDE™

105 #4057

Teddy™
Jade Bear • Born: N/A
Issued: 1994 • Retired: 1995
○ *Got it!* • Paid: $____
Market Value:
a. *New face* – **$500**
b. *Old face* – **$350**

106 #4056

Teddy™
Magenta Bear • Born: N/A
Issued: 1994 • Retired: 1995
○ *Got it!* • Paid: $____
Market Value:
a. *New face* – **$535**
b. *Old face* – **$380**

107 #4051

Teddy™
Teal Bear • Born: N/A
Issued: 1994 • Retired: 1995
○ *Got it!* • Paid: $____
Market Value:
a. *New face* – **$670**
b. *Old face* – **$385**

108 #4055

Teddy™
Violet Bear • Born: N/A
Issued: 1994 • Retired: 1995
○ *Got it!* • Paid: $____
Market Value:
a. *New face* – **$650**
b. *Old face* – **$395**

| Value Totals | _____ |

My Beanie Babies™ Collection

109   #4042

Trap™
Mouse • Born: N/A
Issued: 1994 • Retired: 1996
○ *Got it!* • Paid: $____
Market Value: **$450**

110   #4108

Tuffy™
Terrier • Born: 10-12-96
Issued: 1997 • Current
● *Got it!* • Paid: $____
Market Value: $____

111   #4076

Tusk™
Walrus • Born: 9-18-95
Issued: 1995 • Retired: 1997
○ *Got it!* • Paid: $____
Market Value: **$60**

112   #4068

Twigs™
Giraffe • Born: 5-19-95
Issued: 1996 • Current
● *Got it!* • Paid: $____
Market Value: $____

Value
Totals _____

113   #4058

Valentino™
Bear • Born: 2-14-94
Issued: 1995 • Current
◉ *Got it!* • Paid: $____
Market Value: $____

114   #4064

Retired October 1997

Velvet™
Panther • Born: 12-16-95
Issued: 1995 • ~~Current~~
○ *Got it!* • Paid: $____
Market Value: $_40_

115   #4075

Waddle™
Penguin • Born: 12-19-95
Issued: 1995 • Current
◉ *Got it!* • Paid: $____
Market Value: $____

116   #4084

Waves™
Whale • Born: 12-8-96
Issued: 1997 • Current
◉ *Got it!* • Paid: $____
Market Value: $____

COLLECTOR'S
VALUE GUIDE™

Value
Totals _____

117   #4041

Web™
Spider • Born: N/A
Issued: 1994 • Retired: 1996
○ *Got it!* • Paid: $_____
Market Value: **$575**

118   #4013

Weenie™
Dog • Born: 7-20-95
Issued: 1996 • Current
○ *Got it!* • Paid: $_____
Market Value: $_____

119   #4103

Wrinkles™
Dog • Born: 5-1-96
Issued: 1996 • Current
● *Got it!* • Paid: $_____
Market Value: $_____

120   #4063

Ziggy™
Zebra • Born: 12-24-95
Issued: 1995 • Current
● *Got it!* • Paid: $_____
Market Value: $_____

Value
Totals _____

121 #4004

b

a

c

Zip™
Cat • Born: 3-28-94
Issued: 1994 • Current
Got it! • Paid: $____
Market Value:
a. *Black body/white paws* – $____
b. *All black* – **$1250**
c. *White face & belly* – **$240**

Value
Totals _____

T1 — 4th Release

Chocolate™
Moose • Born: N/A
Issued & Retired: April 1997
🔘 *Got it!* • Paid: $____
Market Value: **$9**

T2 — 3rd Release

Chops™
Lamb • Born: N/A
Issued & Retired: April 1997
🔘 *Got it!* • Paid: $____
Market Value: **$9**

T3 — 5th Release

Goldie™
Goldfish • Born: N/A
Issued & Retired: April 1997
🔘 *Got it!* • Paid: $____
Market Value: **$9**

T4 — 10th Release

Lizz™
Lizard • Born: N/A
Issued & Retired: April 1997
🔘 *Got it!* • Paid: $____
Market Value: **$9**

T5 — 1st Release

Patti™
Platypus • Born: N/A
Issued & Retired: April 1997
🔘 *Got it!* • Paid: $____
Market Value: **$12**

T6 — 2nd Release

Pinky™
Flamingo • Born: N/A
Issued & Retired: April 1997
🔘 *Got it!* • Paid: $____
Market Value: **$15**

Value
Totals _____

COLLECTOR'S
VALUE GUIDE™

T7   9th Release

Quacks™
Duck • Born: N/A
Issued & Retired: April 1997
Got it! • Paid: $____
Market Value: **$9**

T8   7th Release

Seamore™
Seal • Born: N/A
Issued & Retired: April 1997
Got it! • Paid: $____
Market Value: **$9**

T9   8th Release

Snort™
Bull • Born: N/A
Issued & Retired: April 1997
Got it! • Paid: $____
Market Value: **$9**

T10   6th Release

Speedy™
Turtle • Born: N/A
Issued & Retired: April 1997
Got it! • Paid: $____
Market Value: **$9**

COLLECTOR'S
VALUE GUIDE™

Value
Totals _____

Future Releases

1	2	3
4	5	6
7	8	9

Value
Totals _____

10

11

12

13

14

15

16

17

18

COLLECTOR'S
VALUE GUIDE™

Value
Totals _____

Total Value Of My Collection

Value Totals	Value Totals
Page 17 & 16	Page 35
Page 18	Page 36
Page 19	Page 37
Page 20	Page 38
Page 21	Page 39
Page 22	Page 40
Page 23	Page 41
Page 24	Page 42
Page 25	Page 43
Page 26	Page 44
Page 27	Page 45
Page 28	Page 46
Page 29	Page 47
Page 30	Page 48
Page 31	Page 49
Page 32	Page 50
Page 33	Page 51
Page 34	
SUBTOTAL	**SUBTOTAL**

GRAND TOTAL _____

COLLECTOR'S
VALUE GUIDE™

Most of the Beanie Babies collectors out there enjoy Beanie Babies simply because they're so much fun. It would be next to impossible to walk past a shelf of Beanies and not find at least one you want to take home with you! But now that Beanies have made the leap from toy to collectible, there is another exciting aspect to Beanie Babies: secondary market value.

The Beanie Babies secondary market works a little bit differently than that of other collectibles. For most collectibles, secondary market demand is created when pieces are retired, that is, removed from production, and are no longer available in retail stores. As time goes on and the piece becomes less and less available, demand for the piece increases and, *voila* - it acquires a secondary market value.

But there's an interesting twist with Beanie Babies. Because of the huge demand for (and shortage of) *all* Beanies, collectors have begun buying and selling even currently available Beanies at inflated prices. Effectively, this creates a "secondary market" value for current Beanies! Patience will often work to your advantage when shopping for currently available pieces, as you may find a piece being sold for $20, retailing elsewhere for under $10. No matter how desperate collectors are for a given piece, they should always be cautious when shopping the secondary market.

Generally, the most valuable pieces are the older retired Beanies and early variations of existing pieces. Because Beanie Babies fever didn't hit immediately, many early designs came and went without anyone paying much attention. Now that the fever is full-blown, these pieces are highly sought after.

In some cases, pieces may have been produced for only a short time before retiring, thus limiting the available supply. Sometimes production problems are the culprit: "Bronty" the brontosaurus couldn't "hold his beanies" thanks to weak stitching, which means there are a lot fewer surviving "Bronty" pieces than were originally produced.

Secondary Market Overview

Of course, no Beanie Babies will be worth very much unless they're in good condition. This is a tricky issue with Beanie Babies, since it's hard to resist playing with them – after all, that is what they were intended for. The good news is that Beanie Babies can be surface washed (careful, they do not particularly like washing machines!). Many collectors will buy two of the same Beanie when they go shopping; one to store away for "value," the other to use for "play." That way they have the best of both worlds. A note to collectors interested in secondary market values: some people consider Beanie Babies without their hang tags attached (and Teenie Beanies without their sealed protective bags) to be less valuable.

There are several ways you can buy and sell Beanie Babies on the secondary market. One way is to contact your local **retailer**. He or she may have retired Beanies for sale or may be willing to buy your own valuable Beanies. Ask your retailer about **swap & sell** meets in your area. These are events where Beanie enthusiasts get together and, well, swap and sell! You can also place a **classified ad** in your local newspaper in the "collectibles/antiques" section.

But the best way to contact other collectors is via the **Internet**. You really have no idea how impressive the Beanie Babies market is until you surf the web! There are literally hundreds of retailers and collectors who have websites devoted to these adorable animals, in addition to the official Ty website (*www.ty.com*). On the Internet, collectors can make use of on-line price listings, which is a good way to keep up with rapidly changing market trends as they are frequently updated. Collectors can buy, sell or trade whether it's through e-mail or by getting into a "swap and sell" board – there's no shortage of options for the Beanie Babies collector! In addition to secondary market information, collectors can also find a lot of general information on Beanie Babies as well.

With this wealth of information comes a wealth of options. It's best to look around before committing to buying a piece. Ultimately, Beanie Babies will be worth only as much as collectors are willing to pay for them!

COLLECTOR'S
VALUE GUIDE™

Whether due to production errors or design changes, Beanie Babies variations have become a big part of the secondary market. Changes in color are the most common variation, but many Beanies also have had design changes ("Quackers" produced with and without wings) or production errors resulting in abnormalities ("Inky" with nine tentacles, "Radar" with one leg and "Libearty" or "Righty" with missing or upside-down flags). Errors in the hang tags and tush tags are exceedingly frequent, some of which include misprints in birthdates and poems (see examples below) or the misspelling of the name, as with the variations "Ouacker" and "Tuck."

Birthdate Variation   Poem Variation

For some collectors, variations are more than just interesting "curiosities" – they are valuable and rare pieces that are well worth hunting out at stores, swap and sells or the Internet. Some of these variations fetch high prices on the secondary market, although it's up to each collector to decide what a particular variation is really worth to them. Before paying a higher price for an incorrect name on a tag, such as the well-known "swap" of the "Echo" and "Waves" hang tags, remember that tags can easily be detached and reattached on a different piece. The following section details several noteworthy variations.

BONGO/NANA

This Beanie was originally named "Nana." "Nana" looks exactly like the early versions of "Bongo" (with a dark brown tail) except it has a sticker on the hang tag with the name "Bongo" covering up "Nana." "Bongo" was produced with the dark brown tail until early 1996, when the color of his tail became tan to match his face and hands.

Brown tail   Tan tail

Variations

CUBBIE/BROWNIE
The brown bear "Cubbie" was first introduced under a different name – "Brownie." The only difference between the two bears is the name on the hang tag. There is no indication as to how many "Brownie" pieces were produced.

DERBY
Originally produced with its mane and tail made of fine yarn, Derby was revised in 1996 with the mane and tail made from much coarser strands of yarn.

Fine mane
& tail

Coarse mane
& tail

DIGGER
When introduced in 1995, "Digger" was actually colored orange. She changed to her now-familiar red later that year.

Orange

Red

HAPPY
This happy hippo wasn't always the bright and cheery lavender color he is now. When first introduced in the spring of 1995, "Happy" was gray in appearance, but this lasted only until the middle of 1995.

Gray

Lavender

INCH
"Inch" first wormed his way into stores with black felt antennae, but in 1996, he felt it was time for a change and re-emerged with black yarn antennae.

Felt antennae

Yarn antennae

INKY
In the fall of 1994, "Inky" squirmed into town a tan color but by 1995, he had taken on the bright pink hue collectors can spot a mile away!

Tan   Pink

LIZZY
Originally, "Lizzy" was introduced with a tie-dye design. By 1996, she changed to a blue coat with black spots and a yellow belly with orange spots.

Tie-dye   Blue/yellow

LUCKY
When "Lucky" was first issued in 1994, her seven spots were made of felt and glued onto her back. In time the spots tended to fall off, so eventually they were made part of the fabric design. At this time, the spots increased from the original seven, to 11 and then 21. Currently produced pieces have reverted to version two, with 11 spots. Finding an old "Lucky" with all seven of its glued spots intact would be very lucky indeed!

7 glued-on spots   21 sewn-on spots   11 sewn-on spots

MAGIC
The thread in this dragon's wings was initially pale pink, but was later changed to hot pink. Current pieces are being produced once again with the pale pink thread.

Hot pink thread   Pale pink thread

MAPLE
In yet another case of a tag variation resulting in an "identity crisis," the Canadian bear "Maple" has been found with the name "Pride" written on his tush tag.

Variations

MYSTIC

Originally introduced with a white mane and tail of coarse yarn, "Mystic" was issued for six months in 1995 with a mane and tail of fine yarn. Current production has reverted back to the use of coarse yarn.

Fine mane & tail   Coarse mane & tail

NIP

"Nip" has been produced in three different versions. When first issued in 1994, "Nip" had a gold body with a white belly and face. Later he was

produced with an all gold body until mid 1995, when "Nip" featured a gold body, white paws and the addition of a gold ring around his eyes.

White belly & face   All gold   Gold body/ white paws

PATTI

"Patti" has been produced in two different colors, though shading variations among dyes may give the appearance of a variety of different hues.

She first appeared as purple but only for a short time; she was then changed to magenta but has recently reverted back to her original purple.

Magenta   Purple

PEANUT

In one of the most radical examples of color change, "Peanut" was first mistakenly produced as a dark blue for one month in 1995. Her color was then changed to the light blue that she was intended to be all along.

Dark blue   Light blue

QUACKERS

When he was first issued in 1994, poor "Quackers" didn't have any wings! It wasn't long, though, before "Quackers" gained his wings in order to help him keep his balance.

Without wings   With wings

SLY

Don't be fooled by this clever little guy! He first appeared in early 1996 with a white patch on his belly, but by mid-year the patch was gone and "Sly" was all brown. Very sneaky!

White belly   Brown belly

STRUT/DOODLE

Produced for the last few months as "Doodle," the rooster's name has recently changed to "Strut." While there is no confirmed reason for the switch, rumors point to a possible copyright conflict. The name was the only thing that changed and newly-produced versions do not show any design alterations.

SPOOKY

The only ghost in the Beanie Babies collection has appeared with the name "Spook" on the tag instead of "Spooky." Plus, "Spooky" has appeared with three

V-shape   Full-smile   Half-smile

different mouth styles: a v-shape, a full-smile and a half-smile. These beaming variations have generally not affected the value of "Spooky."

SPOT

In the most ironic variation yet, "Spot" the dog was originally produced *without* the black spot on his back. Maybe his name should have been "*Spotless!*"

Without   With spot
spot   on back

Variations

STRIPES

The current version of "Stripes" has a light orange color, but the tiger was also produced in two other versions. When first issued, "Stripes" was a darker orange with wide stripes and had a belly made of fuzzy material; in the next version, he was still dark orange, but his stripes were narrower and his belly was the same plush material as the rest of his body.

Dark orange/
fuzzy belly   Dark orange   Light orange

TANK

Three versions of "Tank" have rolled through the Beanie Babies collection. He first appeared with seven plates on his back; later, he sported nine plates. Today, "Tank" has a shell on his back with nine plates in it, as well as ears on the top, instead of on the side of his head.

7 plates,
no shell   9 plates,
no shell   9 plates,
with shell

TEDDY

Each "Teddy" Beanie – brown, cranberry, jade, magenta, teal and violet – has been produced with two face designs. When first issued, their snouts were pointed; later, their eyes were moved closer together and the snouts had a more rounded appearance. The new face teddies also donned neck ribbons.

Old face   New face

ZIP

"Zip" was first produced with a white face and belly, then his coat changed to all black. The third and current version is all black except for white paws and has the addition of a green rim around the eyes.

White face
& belly   All black   Black body/
white paws

The following are the four Ty hang tags produced to date. Beanie Babies are no longer produced with the first, second and third generation of tags.

The first of the Ty hang tags was a single heart with the original thin Ty logo on the front and style number, name and Ty information on the back.

The second version of the tag had the same Ty logo as the first, but was issued in a folded "booklet" format consisting of two attached hearts. In addition to the style number, name and Ty information, this tag introduced the "To:/From:" section for gift givers.

The third generation of tags pictured an "inflated" Ty logo and featured the same inside information as the second version Ty tag.

The fourth and current version of the tag also features the wider lettering on the Ty logo, with the addition of a yellow star indicating it's an "Original Beanie Baby." This is the first tag to include the birthdate and poem, as well as the Ty website address.

Ty also has produced four generations of body or "tush" tags. Many of these tags can be used to tell the estimated year of production. Like the hang tags, they have undergone many changes including switching from red to black ink, the addition of the Beanie Babies' name and, on the fourth generation tag, the appearance of a red star next to the Ty logo.

Beanie Babies™ Poems

Since early 1996, Ty has included poems on the Beanie Babies' hang tags. Many tags have variations in spelling, punctuation or even wording! See if your Beanie Babies' poems match these official Ty poems. Beanies which stopped production prior to 1996 were never assigned a poem. Have some fun and create your own!

Ally™

When Ally gets out of classes
He wears a hat and dark glasses
He plays bass in a street band
He's the coolest gator in the land!

Baldy™

Hair on his head is quite scant
We suggest Baldy get a transplant
Watching over the land of the free
Hair in his eyes would make it hard to see!

Bernie™

This little dog can't wait to grow
To rescue people lost in the snow
Don't let him out – keep him on your shelf
He doesn't know how to rescue himself!

Bessie™

Bessie the cow likes to dance and sing
Because music is her favorite thing
Every night when you are counting sheep
She'll sing you a song to help you sleep!

Blackie™

Living in a national park
He only played after dark
Then he met his friend Cubbie
Now they play when it's sunny!

Blizzard™

In the mountains, where it's snowy and cold
Lives a beautiful tiger, I've been told
Black and white, she's hard to compare
Of all the tigers, she is most rare!

Bones™

Bones is a dog that loves to chew
Chairs and tables and a smelly old shoe
"You're so destructive" all would shout
But that all stopped, when his teeth
Fell out!

Bongo™

Bongo the monkey lives in a tree
The happiest monkey you'll ever see
In his spare time he plays the guitar
One of these days he will be a big star!

Bronty™

No Poem

_____
_____
_____
_____

Brownie™

No Poem

_____
_____
_____

Bubbles™

All day long Bubbles likes to swim
She never gets tired of flapping her fins
Bubbles lived in a sea of blue
Now she is ready to come home with you!

Bucky™

Bucky's teeth are as shiny as can be
Often used for cutting trees
He hides in his dam night and day
Maybe for you he will come out and play!

COLLECTOR'S
VALUE GUIDE™

Beanie Babies™ Poems

Bumble™

Bumble the bee will not sting you
It is only love that this bee will bring you
So don't be afraid to give this bee a hug
Because Bumble the bee is a love-bug.

Caw™

No Poem

_____
_____
_____
_____

Chilly™

No Poem

_____
_____
_____
_____

Chip™

Black and gold, brown and white
The shades of her coat are quite a sight
At mixing her colors she was a master
On anyone else it would be a disaster!

Chocolate™

Licorice, gum and peppermint candy
This moose always has these handy
There is one more thing he likes to eat
Can you guess his favorite sweet?

Chops™

Chops is a little lamb
This lamb you'll surely know
Because every path that you may take
This lamb is sure to go!

Claude™

Claude the crab paints by the sea
A famous artist he hopes to be
But the tide came in and his paints fell
Now his art is on his shell!

Congo™

Black as the night and fierce is he
On the ground or in a tree
Strong and mighty as the Congo
He's related to our Bongo!

Coral™

Coral is beautiful, as you know
Made of colors in the rainbow
Whether it's pink, yellow or blue
These colors were chosen just for you!

Crunch™

What's for breakfast? What's for lunch?
Yum! Delicious! Munch, munch, munch!
He's eating everything by the bunch
That's the reason we named him Crunch!

Cubbie™

Cubbie used to eat crackers and honey
And what happened to him was funny
He was stung by fourteen bees
Now Cubbie eats broccoli and cheese!

Curly™

A bear so cute with hair that's Curly
You will love and want him surely
To this bear always be true
He will be a friend to you!

Daisy™

Daisy drinks milk each night
So her coat is shiny and bright
Milk is good for your hair and skin
What a way for your day to begin!

Derby™

All the other horses used to tattle
Because Derby never wore his saddle
He left the stables, and the horses too
Just so Derby can be with you!

Beanie Babies™ Poems

Digger™

Digging in the sand and walking sideways
That's how Digger spends her days
Hard on the outside but sweet deep inside
Basking in the sun and riding the tide!

Doby™

This dog is little but he has might
Keep him close when you sleep at night
He lays around with nothing to do
Until he sees it's time to protect you!

Doodle™

Listen closely to "cock-a-doodle-doo"
What's the rooster saying to you?
Hurry, wake up sleepy head
We have lots to do, get out of bed!

Dotty™

The Beanies all thought it was a big joke
While writing her tag, their ink pen broke
She got in the way, and got all spotty
So now the Beanies call her Dotty!

Ears™

He's been eating carrots so long
Didn't understand what was wrong
Couldn't see the board during classes
Until the doctor gave him glasses!

Echo™

Echo the dolphin lives in the sea
Playing with her friends, like you and me
Through the waves she echoes the sound
"I'm so glad to have you around!"

Flash™

You know dolphins are a smart breed
Our friend Flash knows how to read
Splash the whale is the one who taught her
Although reading is difficult under the water!

Fleece™
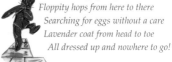
Fleece would like to sing a lullaby
But please be patient, she's rather shy
When you sleep, keep her by your ear
Her song will leave you nothing to fear.

Flip™

Flip the cat is an acrobat
She loves playing on her mat
This cat flips with such grace and flair
She can somersault in mid air!

Floppity™

Floppity hops from here to there
Searching for eggs without a care
Lavender coat from head to toe
All dressed up and nowhere to go!

Flutter™

No Poem
_____
_____
_____
_____

Freckles™

From the trees he hunts prey
In the night and in the day
He's the king of camouflage
Look real close, he's no mirage!

Garcia™
The Beanies use to follow him around
Because Garcia traveled from town to town
He's pretty popular as you can see
Some even say he's legendary!

Goldie™
She's got rhythm, she's got soul
What more to like in a fish bowl?
Through sound waves Goldie swam
Because this goldfish likes to jam!

THE COLLECTOR'S
POCKET PLANNER™

Detach, fold, insert
in vinyl sleeve and
– presto! – you have your
handy pocket planner!

This free pocket
planner is a Beanie
collector's best friend!

Tear here, then fold to create your very own pocket planner!

Winter 1998 Edition

The Collector's Pocket Planner™

Ty®'s Beanie Babies™

A Personal Checklist

Collector's Name

$2.95

---

⑤

My Collection

Want it! / Got it!

- ○ ○ Velvet™, *black panther*
- ○ ○ Waddle™, *black/white penguin*
- ○ ○ Waves™, *black/white orca whale*
- ○ ○ Web™, *black spider*
- ○ ○ Weenie™, *brown dachshund*
- ○ ○ Wrinkles™, *brown/white bulldog*
- ○ ○ Ziggy™, *black/white zebra*
- ○ ○ Zip™, *black cat* †

My Teenie Collection △

- ○ Chocolate™, *brown moose*
- ○ Chops™, *white lamb*
- ○ Goldie™, *orange goldfish*
- ○ Lizz™, *multi-color lizard*
- ○ Patti™, *purple platypus*
- ○ Pinky™, *pink flamingo*
- ○ Quacks™, *yellow duck*
- ○ Seamore™, *white seal*
- ○ Snort™, *red bull*
- ○ Speedy™, *green turtle*

△ available only through special
McDonald's promotion

Copyright © 1997 by Collectors' Publishing Co., Inc.
598 Pomeroy Avenue, Meriden, CT 06450

Visit us on the world wide web:

http://www.collectorspub.com

---

④

My Collection

Want it! / Got it!

- ○ ○ Sly™, *brown fox* †
- ○ ○ Snip™, *brown/cream cat*
- ○ ○ Snort™, *red bull*
- ○ ○ Snowball™, *white snowman*
- ○ ○ Sparky™, *black/white dalmatian*
- ○ ○ Speedy™, *green turtle*
- ○ ○ Spike™, *gray rhinoceros*
- ○ ○ Spinner™, *black/orange spider*
- ○ ○ Splash™, *black/white orca whale*
- ○ ○ Spooky™, *white ghost* †
- ○ ○ Spot™, *black/white dog* †
- ○ ○ Squealer™, *pink pig*
- ○ ○ Steg™, *tie-dye stegosaurus*
- ○ ○ Sting™, *blue/green tie-dye manta ray*
- ○ ○ Stinky™, *black/white skunk*
- ○ ○ Stripes™, *black/orange tiger* †
- ○ ○ Strut™, *tie-dye rooster* †
- ○ ○ Tabasco™, *red bull*
- ○ ○ Tank™, *gray armadillo* †
- ○ ○ Teddy™, *brown bear* †
- ○ ○ Teddy™, *cranberry bear* †
- ○ ○ Teddy™, *jade bear* †
- ○ ○ Teddy™, *magenta bear* †
- ○ ○ Teddy™, *teal bear* †
- ○ ○ Teddy™, *violet bear* †
- ○ ○ Trap™, *gray mouse*
- ○ ○ Tuffy™, *brown terrier*
- ○ ○ Tusk™, *brown walrus*
- ○ ○ Twigs™, *orange giraffe*
- ○ ○ Valentino™, *white bear with heart*

Want it! Got it!

- ○ ○ 1997 Teddy™, *brown holiday bear*
- ○ ○ Ally™, *green alligator*
- ○ ○ Baldy™, *brown/white eagle*
- ○ ○ Batty™, *pink bat*
- ○ ○ Bernie™, *brown St. Bernard*
- ○ ○ Bessie™, *brown/white cow*
- ○ ○ Blackie™, *black bear*
- ○ ○ Blizzard™, *white/black tiger*
- ○ ○ Bones™, *brown dog*
- ○ ○ Bongo™, *brown monkey* †
- ○ ○ Bronty™, *blue tie-dye brontosaurus*
- ○ ○ Brownie™, *brown bear*
- ○ ○ Bubbles™, *black/yellow tropical fish*
- ○ ○ Bucky™, *brown beaver*
- ○ ○ Bumble™, *black/yellow bee*
- ○ ○ Caw™, *black crow*
- ○ ○ Chilly™, *white polar bear*
- ○ ○ Chip™, *black/orange/white cat*
- ○ ○ Chocolate™, *brown moose*
- ○ ○ Chops™, *white lamb*
- ○ ○ Claude™, *tie-dye crab*
- ○ ○ Congo™, *black gorilla*
- ○ ○ Coral™, *tie-dye tropical fish*
- ○ ○ Crunch™, *gray shark*
- ○ ○ Cubbie™, *brown bear* †
- ○ ○ Curly™, *brown bear*
- ○ ○ Daisy™, *black/white cow* †
- ○ ○ Derby™, *brown horse* †

† for variations of this piece, see Value Guide
retired and out of production pieces listed in magenta type

Want it! Got it!

- ○ ○ Digger™, *red crab* †
- ○ ○ Doby™, *black/brown doberman*
- ○ ○ Doodle™, *tie-dye rooster*
- ○ ○ Dotty™, *black/white dalmatian*
- ○ ○ Ears™, *brown bunny*
- ○ ○ Echo™, *gray/white dolphin*
- ○ ○ Flash™, *gray dolphin*
- ○ ○ Fleece™, *white lamb*
- ○ ○ Flip™, *white cat*
- ○ ○ Floppity™, *lavender bunny*
- ○ ○ Flutter™, *tie-dye butterfly*
- ○ ○ Freckles™, *white/orange leopard*
- ○ ○ Garcia™, *tie-dye bear*
- ○ ○ Gobbles™, *brown/red turkey*
- ○ ○ Goldie™, *orange goldfish*
- ○ ○ Gracie™, *white swan*
- ○ ○ Grunt™, *red razorback*
- ○ ○ Happy™, *lavender hippo* †
- ○ ○ Hippity™, *mint green bunny*
- ○ ○ Hoot™, *brown owl*
- ○ ○ Hoppity™, *pink bunny*
- ○ ○ Humphrey™, *brown camel*
- ○ ○ Inch™, *multi-color worm* †
- ○ ○ Inky™, *pink octopus* †
- ○ ○ Jolly™, *brown walrus*
- ○ ○ Kiwi™, *multi-color toucan*
- ○ ○ Lefty™, *blue donkey with U.S. flag*
- ○ ○ Legs™, *green frog*
- ○ ○ Libearty™, *white bear with U.S. flag*
- ○ ○ Lizzy™, *multi-color lizard* †

Want it! Got it!

- ○ ○ Lucky™, *red ladybug* †
- ○ ○ Magic™, *white dragon* †
- ○ ○ Manny™, *gray manatee*
- ○ ○ Maple™, *white bear w/ Canadian flag* †
- ○ ○ Mel™, *gray/white koala*
- ○ ○ Mystic™, *white unicorn* †
- ○ ○ Nana™, *brown monkey*
- ○ ○ Nanook™, *gray/white husky*
- ○ ○ Nip™, *gold cat* †
- ○ ○ Nuts™, *brown squirrel*
- ○ ○ Patti™, *purple platypus* †
- ○ ○ Peace™, *tie-dye bear*
- ○ ○ Peanut™, *blue elephant* †
- ○ ○ Peking™, *black/white panda*
- ○ ○ Pinchers™, *red lobster*
- ○ ○ Pinky™, *pink flamingo*
- ○ ○ Pouch™, *brown kangaroo*
- ○ ○ Pugsly™, *black/cream pug*
- ○ ○ Quackers™, *yellow duck* †
- ○ ○ Radar™, *black bat* †
- ○ ○ Rex™, *tie-dye tyrannosaurus*
- ○ ○ Righty™, *gray elephant with U.S. flag*
- ○ ○ Ringo™, *brown raccoon*
- ○ ○ Roary™, *brown lion*
- ○ ○ Rover™, *red dog*
- ○ ○ Scoop™, *blue pelican*
- ○ ○ Scottie™, *black Scottish Terrier*
- ○ ○ Seamore™, *white seal*
- ○ ○ Seaweed™, *brown otter*
- ○ ○ Slither™, *brown/yellow snake*

Beanie Babies™ Poems

Gracie™

As a duckling, she was confused,
Birds on the lake were quite amused.
Poking fun until she would cry,
Now the most beautiful swan at Ty!

Inch™

Inch the worm is a friend of mine
He goes so slow all the time
Inching around from here to there
Traveling the world without a care!

Grunt™

Some Beanies think Grunt is tough
No surprise, he's scary enough
But if you take him home you'll see
Grunt is the sweetest Beanie Baby!

Inky™

Inky's head is big and round
As he swims he makes no sound
If you need a hand, don't hesitate
Inky can help because he has eight!

Happy™

Happy the Hippo loves to wade
In the river and in the shade
When Happy shoots water out of his snout
You know he's happy without a doubt!

Jolly™

Jolly the walrus is not very serious
He laughs and laughs until he's delirious
He often reminds me of my dad
Always happy, never sad!

Hippity™
Hippity is a cute little bunny
Dressed in green, he looks quite funny
Twitching his nose in the air
Sniffing a flower here and there!

Kiwi™
Kiwi waits for the April showers
Watching a garden bloom with flowers
There trees grow with fruit that's sweet
I'm sure you'll guess his favorite treat!

Hoot™
Late to bed, late to rise
Nevertheless, Hoot's quite wise
Studies by candlelight, nothing new
Like a president, do you know Whooo?

Lefty™
Donkeys to the left, elephants to the right
Often seems like a crazy sight
This whole game seems very funny
Until you realize they're spending
Your money!

Hoppity™
Hopscotch is what she likes to play
If you don't join in, she'll hop away
So play a game if you have the time,
She likes to play, rain or shine!

Legs™

Legs lives in a hollow log
Legs likes to play leap frog
If you like to hang out at the lake
Legs will be the new friend you'll make!

Humphrey™
No Poem
_____
_____
_____
_____

Libearty™

I am called libearty
I wear the flag for all to see
Hope and freedom is my way
That's why I wear flag USA

Beanie Babies™ Poems

Lizzy™

Lizzy loves Legs the frog
    She hides with him under logs
    Both of them search for flies
    Underneath the clear blue skies!

Lucky™

Lucky the lady bug loves the lotto
    "Someone must win" that's her motto
    But save your dimes and even a penny
    Don't spend on the lotto and
You'll have many!

Magic™

Magic the dragon lives in a dream
    The most beautiful that you have ever seen
    Through magic lands she likes to fly
    Look up and watch her, way up high!

Manny™

Manny is sometimes called a sea cow
    She likes to twirl and likes to bow
    Manny sure is glad you bought her
    Because it's so lonely under water!

Maple™

Maple the bear likes to ski
    With his friends, he plays hockey.
    He loves his pancakes and eats every crumb
    Can you guess which country he's from?

Mel™

How do you name a Koala bear?
    It's rather tough, I do declare!
    It confuses me, I get into a funk
    I'll name him Mel, after my favorite hunk!

Mystic™

Once upon a time so far away
    A unicorn was born one day in May
    Keep Mystic with you, she's a prize
    You'll see the magic in her blue eyes!

Nana™

No Poem

_____
_____
_____
_____

Nanook™

Nanook is a dog that loves cold weather
    To him a sled is light as a feather
    Over the snow and through the slush
    He runs at hearing the cry of "mush"!

Nip™

His name is Nipper, but we call him Nip
    His best friend is a black cat named Zip
    Nip likes to run in races for fun
    He runs so fast he's always number one!

Nuts™

With his bushy tail, he'll scamper up a tree
    The most cheerful critter you'll ever see,
    He's nuts about nuts, and he loves to chat
    Have you ever seen a squirrel like that?

Patti™

Ran into Patti one day while walking
    Believe me she wouldn't stop talking
    Listened and listened to her speak
    That would explain her extra large beak!

Peace™

All races, all colors, under the sun
    Join hands together and have some fun
    Dance to the music, rock and roll is the sound
Symbols of peace and love abound!

Peanut™

Peanut the elephant walks on tip-toes
    Quietly sneaking wherever she goes
    She'll sneak up on you and a hug
    You will get
    Peanut is a friend you won't soon forget!

Beanie Babies™ Poems

Peking™

No Poem
_____
_____
_____

Rex™

No Poem
_____
_____
_____

Pinchers™

This lobster loves to pinch
Eating his food inch by inch
Balancing carefully with his tail
Moving forward slow as a snail!

Righty™

Donkeys to the left, elephants to the right
Often seems like a crazy sight
This whole game seems very funny
Until you realize they're spending
Your money!

Pinky™

Pinky loves the everglades
From the hottest pink she's made
With floppy legs and big orange beak
She's the Beanie that you seek!

Ringo™

Ringo hides behind his mask
He will come out, if you should ask
He loves to chitter. He loves to chatter
Just about anything, it doesn't matter!

Pouch™

My little pouch is handy I've found
It helps me carry my baby around
I hop up and down without any fear
Knowing my baby is safe and near.

Roary™

Deep in the jungle they crowned him king
But being brave is not his thing
A cowardly lion some may say
He hears his roar and runs away!

Pugsly™

Pugsly is picky about what he will wear
Never a spot, a stain or a tear
Image is something of which he'll gloat
Until he noticed his wrinkled coat!

Rover™

This dog is red and his name is Rover
If you call him he is sure to come over
He barks and plays with all his might
But worry not, he won't bite!

Quackers™
There is a duck by the name of Quackers
Every night he eats animal crackers
He swims in a lake that's clear and blue
But he'll come to the shore to be with you!

Scoop™
All day long he scoops up fish
To fill his bill, is his wish
Diving fast and diving low
Hoping those fish are very slow!

Radar™
Radar the bat flies late at night
He can soar to an amazing height
If you see something as high as a star
Take a good look, it might be Radar!

Scottie™
Scottie is a friendly sort
Even though his legs are short
He is always happy as can be
His best friends are you and me!

COLLECTOR'S
VALUE GUIDE™

Beanie Babies™ Poems

Seamore™

Seamore is a little white seal
Fish and clams are her favorite meal
Playing and laughing in the sand
She's the happiest seal in the land!

Seaweed™

Seaweed is what she likes to eat
It's supposed to be a delicious treat
Have you tried a treat from the water
If you haven't, maybe you "otter"!

Slither™

No Poem
_____
_____
_____

Sly™

Sly is a fox and tricky is he
Please don't chase him, let him be
If you want him, just say when
He'll peek out from his den!

Snip™

Snip the cat is Siamese
She'll be your friend if you please
So toss her a toy or a piece of string
Playing with you is her favorite thing!

Snort™

Although Snort is not so tall
He loves to play basketball
He is a star player in his dreams
Can you guess his favorite team?

Sparky™

Sparky rides proud on the fire truck
Ringing the bell and pushing his luck
He gets under foot when trying to help
He often gets stepped on and
Lets out a yelp!

Speedy™

Speedy ran marathons in the past
Such a shame, always last
Now Speedy is a big star
After he bought a racing car!

Spike™

Spike the rhino likes to stampede
He's the bruiser that you need
Gentle to birds on his back and spike
You can be his friend if you like!

Splash™

Splash loves to jump and dive
He's the fastest whale alive
He always wins the 100 yard dash
With a victory jump he'll make a splash!

Spooky™

Ghosts can be a scary sight
But don't let Spooky bring you any fright
Because when you're alone, you will see
The best friend that Spooky can be!

Spot™

See Spot sprint, see Spot run
You and Spot will have lots of fun
Watch out now, because he's not slow
Just stand back and watch him go!

Squealer™

Squealer likes to joke around
He is known as class clown
Listen to his stories awhile
There is no doubt he'll make you smile!

Steg™

No Poem
_____
_____
_____

Beanie Babies™ Poems

Sting™

I'm a manta ray and my name is Sting
I'm quite unusual and this is the thing
Under the water I glide like a bird
Have you ever seen something so absurd?

Stinky™

Deep in the woods he lived in a cave
Perfume and mints were the gifts he gave
He showered every night in the kitchen sink
Hoping one day he wouldn't stink!

Stripes™

Stripes was never fierce nor strong
So with tigers, he didn't get along
Jungle life was hard to get by
So he came to his friends at Ty!

Strut™

Listen closely to "cock-a-doodle-doo"
What's the rooster saying to you?
Hurry, wake up sleepy head
We have lots to do, get out of bed!

Tabasco™

Although Tabasco is not so tall
He loves to play basketball
He is a star player in his dream
Can you guess his favorite team?

Tank™

This armadillo lives in the South
Shoving Tex-Mex in his mouth
He sure loves it south of the border
Keeping his friends in good order!

Teddy™ (brown)

Teddy wanted to go out today
All of his friends went out to play
But he'd rather help whatever you do
After all, his best friend is you!

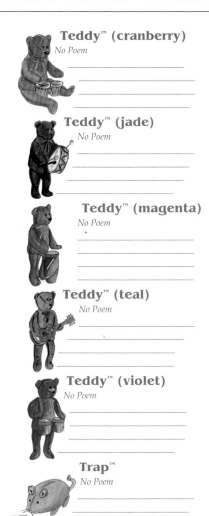

Teddy™ (cranberry)

No Poem

_____
_____
_____
_____

Teddy™ (jade)

No Poem

_____
_____
_____

Teddy™ (magenta)

No Poem

•
_____
_____
_____
_____

Teddy™ (teal)

No Poem

_____
_____
_____

Teddy™ (violet)

No Poem

_____
_____
_____
_____

Trap™

No Poem

_____
_____
_____

Tuffy™

Taking off with a thunderous blast
Tuffy rides his motorcycle fast
The Beanies roll with laughs and squeals
He never took off his training wheels!

Beanie Babies™ Poems

Tusk™
Tusk brushes his teeth everyday
To keep them shiny, it's the only way
Teeth are special, so you must try
And they will sparkle when
You say "Hi"!

Twigs™

Twigs has his head in the clouds
He stands tall, he stands proud
With legs so skinny they wobble and shake
What an unusual friend he will make!

Valentino™
His heart is red and full of love
He cares for you so give him a hug
Keep him close when feeling blue
Feel the love he has for you!

Velvet™

Velvet loves to sleep in the trees
Lulled to dreams by the buzz of the bees
She snoozes all day and plays all night
Running and jumping in the moonlight!

Waddle™
Waddle the Penguin likes to dress up
Every night he wears his tux
When Waddle walks, it never fails
He always trips over his tails!

Waves™
Join him today on the Internet
Don't be afraid to get your feet wet
He taught all the Beanies how to surf
Our web page is his home turf!

Web™
No Poem
_____
_____
_____

Weenie™
Weenie the dog is quite a sight
Long of body and short of height
He perches himself high on a log
And considers himself to be top dog!

Wrinkles™
This little dog is named Wrinkles
His nose is soft and often crinkles
Likes to climb up on your lap
He's a cheery sort of chap!

Ziggy™

Ziggy likes soccer – he's a referee
That way he watches the games for free
The other Beanies don't think it's fair
But Ziggy the Zebra doesn't care!

Zip™

Keep Zip by your side all the day through
Zip is good luck, you'll see it's true
When you have something you need to do
Zip will always believe in you!

Beanie Babies™
October 1997 New Releases
Poems not available at press time!

1997 Teddy™   **Batty™**   **Gobbles™**

Snowball™   **Spinner™**

COLLECTOR'S
VALUE GUIDE™

My Beanie Babies™ Record

Collection Diary

Use this page to record the important highlights about your Beanie Babies™ collection.

My First Beanie:

Where I Got It:

When I Got It:

My Favorite Beanie:

Where I Got It:

When I Got It:

My Most Valuable Beanie:

Where I Got It:

When I Got It:

My Hardest-To-Find Beanie:

Where I Got It:

When I Got It:

My Most Wanted Beanies:

COLLECTOR'S
VALUE GUIDE™

Fun & Games

Word Scramble

*Try to rearrange the letters to spell
your favorite Beanie Babies™ names.
Good luck!* (See page 79 for answers)

1. ILRNWSKE _____
2. YPKRSA _____
3. NOANOK _____
4. NTGSI _____
5. PTAR _____
6. LAYL _____
7. SWTGI _____
8. SVEAW _____
9. OPCSO _____
10. LAWSBOLN _____

11. ZLDBRZIA _____
12. NOGOB _____
13. EOSBLGB _____
14. YADSI _____
15. HALFS _____
16. LOEDOD _____
17. ETNVLAION _____
18. COHE _____
19. LPIF _____
20. CAGIRA _____

Word Search

*Find your favorite Beanie Babies™ in this
challenging word search. There are 20 in all. Happy hunting!*

ALLY
ECHO
FLASH
GARCIA
HOOT

NIP
QUACKERS
REX
ROARY
SLY

INCH
INKY
KIWI
MAGIC
NANOOK

SNIP
STEG
TANK
TUFFY
WEB

Q	G	A	R	C	I	A	E	C	H	O
C	U	E	I	N	F	N	K	B	E	W
Y	X	A	C	R	O	L	K	C	S	M
E	O	H	C	O	M	S	L	Y	O	A
A	I	F	O	K	O	O	N	A	N	G
R	P	F	I	O	E	J	Y	I	E	I
S	L	W	L	L	T	R	T	T	S	C
R	I	C	K	A	A	L	S	N	I	P
W	Y	N	E	O	S	Y	A	L	L	Y
D	A	E	R	T	U	H	H	B	D	I
T	U	F	F	Y	R	G	O	N	I	P

Beanie Babies™ Quiz

Try to identify the Beanie Babies™ that are being described in the clues below. Can you get them all?

1. Look for me up in the trees, I love to swing to and fro by my tail (which has been two different colors). If you call me by name, it may take me a minute to answer because I used to have a different name and sometimes I get confused. Who am I?

2. You may not believe in me, but here I am. Don't be tricked, I'm really a treat. I was born on All Hallow's Eve. Who am I?

3. I'm the best dressed of the bunch. When I spread my wings, I soar, but you won't find me in the sky and I'm not so graceful on the ground. Who am I?

4. Some people find me lucky. I would invite you to my home for a housewarming party as I am brand new to the Beanie neighborhood, but I'm afraid you might get tangled up there and would be late for dinner (your dinner). Who am I?

5. My legs are my best feature. You can find me down near the water by my Florida home or sometimes in some people's lawns. I have a teenie friend who looks just like me. Who am I?

6. We're not that easy to find (except for on the big screen). Once we could be seen anywhere sporting our tie-dye and stomping across the land. Who are we?

7. I love to sing, my voice is sweet but not as sugary as my chocolate treat. My birthday is June 27, 1995. Who am I?

(See page 79 for answers)

Beanie Babies™ ID Game

Looking at the picture above, try to find 19 of your favorite Beanie Babies™ playing a game of hide-and-seek. Hint: don't overlook anything! Have a wonderful journey! (See page 79 for answers)

Beanie Babies™ Birthdays

Do you or any of your family and friends share a birthday with your favorite Beanies? Check this handy list to find out!

JANUARY

Jan. 3, 1993 . . . . .Spot
Jan. 6, 1993 . . . . .Patti
Jan. 13, 1996 . . . . .Crunch
Jan. 15, 1996 . . . . . . .Mel
Jan. 18, 1994 . . . . . .Bones
Jan. 21, 1996 . . . . . . .Nuts
Jan. 25, 1995 . . . . .Peanut
Jan. 26, 1996 . . . . . . .Chip

FEBRUARY

Feb. 1, 1996 . . . . . . .Peace
Feb. 13, 1995 . . . . . .Pinky
Feb. 13, 1995 . . . . .Stinky
Feb. 14, 1994 . .Valentino
Feb. 17, 1996 . . . . . .Baldy
Feb. 20, 1996 . . . . . .Roary
Feb. 22, 1995 . . . . . .Tank
Feb. 25, 1994 . . . . .Happy
Feb. 27, 1996 . . . . .Sparky
Feb. 28, 1995 . . . . . . .Flip

MARCH

March 2, 1995 . . . . .Coral
March 6, 1994 . . . . . .Nip
March 8, 1996 . . .Doodle
March 8, 1996 . . . . .Strut
March 14, 1994 . . . . .Ally
March 19, 1996 .Seaweed
March 21, 1996 . . .Fleece
March 28, 1994 . . . . . .Zip

APRIL

April 3, 1996 . . .Hoppity
April 12, 1996 . . . . .Curly
April 18, 1995 . . . . . .Ears
April 19, 1994 .Quackers
April 23, 1993 . .Squealer
April 25, 1993 . . . . . .Legs
April 27, 1993 .Chocolate

MAY

May 1, 1995 . . . . . .Lucky
May 1, 1996 . . .Wrinkles
May 2, 1996 . . . . .Pugsly
May 3, 1996 . . . . . .Chops
May 10, 1994 . . . . .Daisy
May 11, 1995 . . . . . .Lizzy
May 13, 1993 . . . . .Flash
May 15, 1995 . . . . .Snort
May 15, 1995 . . .Tabasco
May 19, 1995 . . . .Twigs
May 21, 1994 . . . . .Mystic
May 28, 1996 . . .Floppity
May 30, 1996 . . . . .Rover

JUNE

June 1, 1996 . . . . .Hippity
June 3, 1996 . . . .Freckles
June 8, 1995 . . . . . .Bucky
June 8, 1995 . . . . .Manny
June 11, 1995 . . . .Stripes
June 15, 1996 . . . .Scottie
June 17, 1996 . . . . .Gracie
June 19, 1993 . . .Pinchers
June 27, 1995 . . . . .Bessie

JULY

July 1, 1996 . . . . . .Maple
July 1, 1996 . . . . . .Scoop
July 2, 1995 . . . .Bubbles
July 4, 1996 . . . . . .Lefty
July 4, 1996 . . . . . .Righty
July 8, 1993 . . . . .Splash
July 14, 1995 . . . . .Ringo
July 15, 1994 . . . .Blackie
July 19, 1995 . . . . .Grunt
July 20, 1995 . . . .Weenie

AUGUST

Aug. 1, 1995 . . . . .Garcia
Aug. 9, 1995 . . . . . . .Hoot
Aug. 13, 1996 . . . . .Spike
Aug. 14, 1994 . . . .Speedy
Aug. 17, 1995 . . . .Bongo
Aug. 23, 1995 . . . .Digger
Aug. 27, 1995 . . . . . .Sting

SEPTEMBER

Sept. 3, 1996 . . . .Claude
Sept. 3, 1995 . . . . . . .Inch
Sept. 5, 1995 . . . . .Magic
Sept. 12, 1996 . . . . . . .Sly
Sept. 16, 1995 . . . .Derby
Sept. 16, 1995 . . . . .Kiwi
Sept. 18, 1995 . . . . . .Tusk

OCTOBER

Oct. 3, 1996 . . . . . .Bernie
Oct. 9, 1996 . . . . . . .Doby
Oct. 12, 1996 . . . . . .Tuffy
Oct. 16, 1995 . . . .Bumble
Oct. 17, 1996 . . . . . .Dotty
Oct. 22, 1996 . . . . . . .Snip
Oct. 28, 1996 . . . .Spinner
Oct. 29, 1996 . . . . . .Batty
Oct. 30, 1995 . . . . .Radar
Oct. 31, 1995 . . .Spooky

NOVEMBER

Nov. 6, 1996 . . . . .Pouch
Nov. 9, 1996 . . . . .Congo
Nov. 14, 1993 . . . .Cubbie
Nov. 14, 1994 . . . .Goldie
Nov. 21, 1996 . . .Nanook
Nov. 27, 1996 . . .Gobbles
Nov. 28, 1995 . . . . .Teddy
Nov. 29, 1994 . . . . . .Inky

DECEMBER

Dec. 2, 1996 . . . . . . .Jolly
Dec. 8, 1996 . . . . . .Waves
Dec. 12, 1996 . . .Blizzard
Dec. 14, 1996 . . .Seamore
Dec. 16, 1995 . . . . .Velvet
Dec. 19, 1995 . . . .Waddle
Dec. 21, 1996 . . . . . .Echo
Dec. 22, 1996 . .Snowball
Dec. 24, 1995 . . . . .Ziggy
Dec. 25, 1996 .1997 Teddy

Remember, some older Beanie Babies and the Teenie Beanie Babies don't have birthdates. It might be fun to create your own!

Ty®'s Pillow Pals™ – Next Big Thing?

PP1 #3008

Ba Ba™
Lamb • Size: 15″
Current
○ *Got it!* • Paid: $____
Market Value: $____

PP2 #3018

Bruiser™
Dog • Size: N/A
Current
○ *Got it!* • Paid: $____
Market Value: $____

PP3 #3010

Carrots™
Bunny • Size: 15″
Current
○ *Got it!* • Paid: $____
Market Value: $____

PP4 #3002

Huggy™
Bear • Size: 15″
Current
○ *Got it!* • Paid: $____
Market Value: $____

PP5 #3011

Meow™
Cat • Size: 15″
Current
○ *Got it!* • Paid: $____
Market Value: $____

PP6 #3004

Moo™
Cow • Size: 15″
Current
○ *Got it!* • Paid: $____
Market Value: $____

PP7 #3005

Oink™
Pig • Size: 15″
Current
○ *Got it!* • Paid: $____
Market Value: $____

PP8 #3016

Purr™
Tiger • Size: 15″
Current
○ *Got it!* • Paid: $____
Market Value: $____

PP9 #3006

Ribbit™
Frog • Size: 14″
Current
○ *Got it!* • Paid: $____
Market Value: $____

Value Totals _____

COLLECTOR'S
VALUE GUIDE™

PP10   #3009

Ribbit™
Frog • Size: 14"
Current
○ *Got it!* • Paid: $____
Market Value: $____

PP11   #3007

Snap™
Turtle • Size: 14"
Current
○ *Got it!* • Paid: $____
Market Value: $____

PP12   #3015

Snap™
Turtle • Size: 14"
Current
○ *Got it!* • Paid: $____
Market Value: $____

PP13   #3001

Snuggy™
Bear • Size: 15"
Current
○ *Got it!* • Paid: $____
Market Value: $____

PP14   #3017

Speckles™
Leopard • Size: 15"
Current
○ *Got it!* • Paid: $____
Market Value: $____

PP15   #3013

Squirt™
Elephant • Size: 15"
Current
○ *Got it!* • Paid: $____
Market Value: $____

PP16   #3012

Tubby™
Hippopotamus • Size: 15"
Current
○ *Got it!* • Paid: $____
Market Value: $____

PP17   #3003

Woof™
Dog • Size: 15"
Current
○ *Got it!* • Paid: $____
Market Value: $____

PP18   #3014

Zulu™
Zebra • Size: 15"
Current
○ *Got it!* • Paid: $____
Market Value: $____

COLLECTOR'S VALUE GUIDE™

Value Totals _____

Index By Animal Type

Alphabetical Index

Fun & Games Answers

Word Scramble (page 74): 1. Wrinkles 2. Sparky 3. Nanook 4. Sting 5. Trap 6. Ally 7. Twigs 8. Waves 9. Scoop 10. Snowball 11. Blizzard 12. Bongo 13. Gobbles 14. Daisy 15. Flash 16. Doodle 17. Valentino 18. Echo 19. Flip 20. Garcia

Beanie Babies™ Quiz (page 75): 1. Bongo 2. Spooky 3. Waddle 4. Spinner 5. Pinky 6. Bronty, Rex and Steg 7. Bessie

Beanie Babies™ ID Game (page 76): Bessie, Chocolate, Crunch, Flutter, Hippity, Hoot, Humphrey, Inch, Inky, Lizzy, Lucky, Magic, Mystic, Patti, Peanut, Ringo, Rover, Scoop, Waddle

Look for these other

COLLECTOR'S
VALUE GUIDE™

titles at fine gift and collectible stores everywhere.

THE
BOYDS COLLECTION LTD.

Department 56®
Villages

Cherished
Teddies®
by ENESCO®

Beanie Babies™

Department 56®
Snowbabies©

HALLMARK
Keepsake Ornaments

by ENESCO

COLLECTORS'
PUBLISHING
598 Pomeroy Ave., Meriden, CT 06450
WEB http://www.collectorspub.com